THE RHYTHM OF LIFE
Poetry

Copyright © 2020 by James Carlton Williams

All Rights Reserved. No part of this book may be used or reproduced by any means, graphic, electronic, or mechanical, including photocopying, recording, taping, or by any information storage retrieval system without the written permission of the publisher except in the case of brief quotations embodied in critical articles and reviews.

Williams and Associates LLC
11639 Hwy 231/431
P.O. Box 441
Meridian, AL 35759

Assisted by: Global Destiny Enterprise, LLC
Cover design by: Angela Mills Camper of Dezign Pro Printing & Graphics
Printed in the United States of America
First Printing, 2020
ISBN: 978-1-7379599-0-0

Contents

Introduction 5

Consciousness

Stop 8
A Silence So Loud 10
Rise Above It 11
Silence Is Violence 12
Show Me 13
I Want My Rights—Right Now 15
I'm a Black Man 17
Black Woman 18
Our Skin Color Goes Deep 20
Mask on, Mask off 22

Faith

God — The First Spoken Word Artist 26
Songbird 27
Making Melody in My Heart 28
No Tears Left for Tomorrow 29
When My Soul Is Quiet 30
Transcendent Love 31
Holy Spirit 32

Struggle

Pieces of Me 34
Life's Struggles 35
The Best Part of Me 36
I Had a Fight with a Man 37
2018 38
Just One Chance 39
Black Friday 41
So Much Better 42

Love

When Two Become One 44
"I do," Again 45
Can Two Walk Together? 46
Today I Saw Love 48
Thinking of You 50
Chocolate Valentine 51
Secrets 52
The Sugar 53
The Answer 54

Family

Family Reunion 58
A Poem Just for You (Monica Copprue) 59
You Taught Me to Be a Dad 61
My Little Princess 63
Your Mother and I 65
Mother Dear (Madea) 66
"My Daddy" 68
Thank You, Brother 70

Relationship

Naked 72
First Impressions 73
Material Stuff 74
What's On Your Mind? 75
Beautiful, Bold, and Confident 76
Someone Like You 77
A Smile as Lovely as a Poem 79

Humor

The Funk Is Real 82
Boy Bye! (Sean Spicer) 84
A Glass of Wine/a Shot/a Keg of Beer 85
People Watching 86

Introduction

Rhythm by definition is a recurrent alternation of strong and weak elements in the flow of sound and silence in speech. In poetry, rhythm can be described as the beat and pace of a poem. I have been writing poetry for more than thirty (30) years and have come to realize that to everything in life, there is a rhythm and a rhyme, like a heartbeat that mirrors the characteristics of poetry. It's a combination of highs and lows, along with the regular beat in between. We all prefer to remain on that regular beat, in our comfort zones because being made to feel uncomfortable is frightening and filled with too many unknowns. But to grow and change in life, we have to break out of those boundaries and feel discomfort. The ebbs and flows of life destroy those boundaries and provide the fertilizer for growth by testing our faith, will, and discipline to survive when we find ourselves in a space we have never been in before. Some of my writings are about my personal life experiences, but many are written about thoughts, ideas, or observations I have seen in my years of living.

By profession, I am technical with a background in Information Technology, Software Engineering, and Computer Information System Security, but I have always felt my creative and artistic abilities are my natural state. Writing poetry gives me the outlet to be creative while expressing my inner feelings about faith, love, social issues, politics, life, and other thoughts. God has given me the ability to write, and I try to do so with clarity. My writings are simple and easy to interpret while in many cases, they address complex issues that are both personal and public. I also explore the broader issues that affect society from the perspective of the Black community. These include some of the influences that are internal to the Black community and the external influences that originate from outside forces, which affect our communities both positively and negatively.

In publishing this book of poetry, I hope a poem or word I have written will inspire and motivate you to tap into your inner thoughts to give you what you need to understand your own rhythm of life.

James Williams

Consciousness

Stop
A Silence So Loud
Rise above It
Silence Is Violence
Show Me
I Want My Rights—Right Now
I'm a Black Man
Black Woman
Our Skin Color Runs Deep
Mask on, Mask off

Stop

Stop calling me "Yo Nigga" cause that's not who I am or want to be
A racist word is racist, though spoken by someone the same color as me

And I don't need to speak Ebonics just to prove that I'm Black
Or wear my baseball cap with the bib flipped toward the back

I don't need to wear my pants sagging below my waistline
You don't need to know I wear boxer briefs or that they're Calvin Klein

Stop passing that garbage off to the world as Black culture
It's good for nothing but to be tossed away as food for the vulture

Stop letting the freedom we died for and fought so hard to gain
Work against us to bind us with the chains of slavery again

Stop with all the excuses; they are the useless tools of the blind
They only keep you bound by the prison of your own closed mind

Stop letting TV define you as a drug dealer, hustler, or thief
You can be whatever you want to be, doctor, lawyer, or Indian chief

Stop giving racism the power to determine our destination
Let's stop it dead in its tracks and put an end to its intimidation

But we can't fight it with the weapons of ignorance and denial
The weapons we must choose are education and a spiritual revival

Our ancestors were determined not to let racism choose their fate
Instead, they chose to rewrite the script that was pre-defined by hate

We too must pave a highway for a future that we design for us
And stop following the path of destruction,
which others have devised for us

Knowledge is the ladder we will need to climb over hate's wall
Without knowledge and wisdom, hate will prevail and destroy us all

So stop with the myth that we can't do
science and engineering that well
Wake up Carver and Banneker and try to tell them that tall tale

Stop getting so caught up with our successes in all of the sports
Though it's great we've excelled on all the arenas and courts

And Serena looks so fine as she conquers Wimbledon's Center Court
But I would love to see a fine sister sit
on the bench of the Supreme Court

As lawyers and judges, we can help
bring about change to unjust laws
Just like Thurgood Marshall succeeded
in clipping off Jim Crow's long claws

We must continue our climb to the
summit of Dr. King's mountain top
The promised land lies ahead for us if only we would stop

A Silence So Loud

Shots ring out; another Black boy is gone
Just 14 years old, not even fully grown

Another Black mother left in pain and sorrow
Her young man dead and won't rise tomorrow

Not shot by a cop but by his own Black brother
Yet another black boy with a grieving Black mother

Two more Black boys' lives are gone forever
Two young Black mothers trying to hold it together

But there's a silence so loud, listen, can you hear it?
Volume turned way up, don't need to be near it

A silence so loud, it makes my eardrums bleed
No protests seen on the around-the-clock newsfeed

No outrage, no marches, no buildings burned to the ground
No witnesses, no activists, no CNN cameramen to be found

Not a single painted sign saying "Black Lives Matter"
Just a stain on the ground of a Black boy's blood splatter

Silence, can you hear it? It's deafening and bold
Why so quiet though silence is like gold?

He that has an ear let him hear what the silence says
We as a people must change our ways

Rise Above It

Why can't we rise above the tide?
Are we to always be cast as the clown?
The vagabond, the wanderer with no place
to lay his head, no place to set his feet. We ourselves
have become the enemy.
What the slave master couldn't do and where Jim Crow failed
we have managed to succeed by perfecting the art of excuse.
It's someone else's fault I didn't succeed.
I could have become wealthy but...
I was almost the best except...
If it had not been for this...
If I get hooked on drugs, it's because
someone put them in my community.
If I get busted for selling drugs, I was entrapped.
If I serve more time for my offense, I was treated unfairly.
If I don't meet the standard, I was discriminated against.
Let's rise above the tide of racism and
be the buoyant vessel we are and were meant to be.
We gamble on sports and entertainment
as the only avenues to success.
Let not the lottery determine your fortune.

Silence Is Violence

I'm caught in this wave of blue, black, and white silence with no
one stepping up to the plate to end the cycle of violence

The law that swore under oath to protect from violence
is the same law that now murders and threatens, then
hides under the cover of the blue code of silence

And our Black community continues to use the
no snitch rule as their go-to play, while they
allow the thugs and criminals to rule the day

And shame on our white friends who say racism is
dead because the KKK no longer wears white robes
and hoodies, but business suits and ties instead

So should I stay mute and suffer in silence, while those
who I think care for me really don't mind if I live or die?

Hell no! I'm gonna scream bloody murder in my loudest
voice until you hear me loud and clear! Trust me;
I'm not going away unless Jesus parts the sky

I thought the color of silence was golden, not
black, white, or blue, but your eyes remain wide
shut and your lips are sealed with super glue

It doesn't really matter the color of silence;
so what if it's painted blue, black, or white?
Silence is still violence in any shade or hue

Until we learn to speak up for ourselves,
the justice we're due will continue to delay
Silence is a debt we can't afford and violence
has a price that's too high to pay

Show Me

If you're sincere that you're not a racist then show me
If you really want to know what I'm about then get to know me

Talk to me, and you'll see our differences
are not so different from each other
Although the color of our skin is different,
we are brothers from the same mother

I'm not a rapist, murderer, thug, or criminal,
so don't prejudge me that way
And I'm more than an athlete you love
on gameday and hate every other day

I'm a husband, father, son, brother,
and a good friend if you allow me to be
In fact, I'm everything you are,
just give me a chance, and you'll see

You try to convince me that racism is dead;
can you tell me why?
Did the racist all move to another country?
Or better yet, did they all die?

The latter I hope since another shouldn't
have the same struggle with your racist ass
For you've saturated the ground with the
blood of my ancestors with your racist acts

You wrap Christianity around your
hatred and preach Jesus is the way
Yet, your actions say something else.

Oh, I forgot; that's always been your go-to play

If that's your vision of love, then I would rather you hate me
Just treat me how you really feel
because I can't fight what I can't see

If you mean it when you say racism is dead,
then stop treating me like your enemy
Since love is the remedy for racist
behavior don't tell me, just show me

I Want My Rights—Right Now

How am I a leftist when I'm just trying to be right where you are and claim the rights that are rightfully mine? Civil, religious, equal, hell—even human rights! Don't I get credit for that one just for being humankind?

Can't I take credit for doing basic human stuff like eating, sleeping, breathing, thinking, or feeling? Can't I fight for my rights like other human beings do by sitting, standing, walking, talking, and kneeling?

"I Am a Man" just like the signs worn by the sanitation workers stated in those black and white photos from the sixties. So call me by the name my mother calls me. Stop calling me "Criminal" "Thug" and "Sons of Bitches"

And why is it that you say your rights are inalienable, while my rights have to come with your consent? When will it be the right time, place, setting, or moment on your time-table for my next historic event?

246 years of oppression, suppression, and torture before you decided I finally had a right to be free. Another 100 years of unjust laws then you decided I'm human enough to have the right be treated equally

It took another 44 years before you elected a Black president: Barack Obama, number forty-four. But only 8 years later, you elected number forty-five and told him to make America great like it was 100 years ago

If wanting to have the same rights as you paints me as being politically correct, then go ahead and color me that. Cause I can change my politics, religion, status, and opinion, but I can't change the fact that my skin color is black

And even if I could change it and enjoy the privileges it brings, black is still the only color I'd ever want to be. I want my rights right now, not on your terms but mine. I don't have another 400 years left, so right now is the right time for me

I'm a Black Man

Why do you look at me with contempt?
Is it because my skin is dark?
For it's the sun that looked on me with
favor and blessed me with this beauty mark

Why do you conspire against me and
pretend my life doesn't matter?
Don't you know that I have the bloodline
of kings and warriors mighty in battle?

Why do you question my intelligence and
my very statue as a man
When you've seen my handiwork around
the world, even in ancient Egyptian sand?

I'm a man just like you and I've had my share
of disappointments, failures, and faults
But why do my sins live forever, while
yours are not given a second thought?

I'm just a man with ambitions, hopes,
and great expectations
Yet, you set boundaries for me that are
products of your prejudiced limitations

Your crafty plans were put in place to
crush my dignity and pride
But like that wayward boat that dwells
in the sea, I'll crest with the rising tide

I'm a Black man, and I've become stronger
by the suffering my eyes have seen
I have been cut down, but I still stand
tall like the cedar tree, evergreen

Black Woman

Black woman, you're more than the
curl in your hair and luscious full lips
Your beauty runs deeper than toned
thighs and the curve of your hips

Black woman, your name is mother of
pearl, crowned jewel of the universe
The whole earth knows your name
and your deeds are written in verse

Black woman, no one can deny the
feelings the vision of you stirs
Your love has helped build kingdoms
and your beauty has stopped worlds

Black woman, you're so fearfully and
wonderfully designed
And the essence of your beauty
dwells in the recesses of my mind

Black woman, more precious than
diamonds, valuable, rare, and fine
Pure carbon transformed into beauty
by the forces of pressure and time

Black woman, your beauty is world-renowned
as being comely and fair
Your passion is shown by the creative ways
in which you style your hair

Black woman, your sun-kissed skin
color is reflective in fifty shades of black
Your beauty never fades and in nothing
does your complexion lack

Black woman, those alluring eyes have
seen our triumph and gain
And with those same eyes, you have
witnessed our suffering and pain

Black woman, words pour from your
lips as an ointment soothing my soul
With those same lips, you pour your
love into me to make me whole

Black woman, my heart is willingly
captured by your love's hidden snare
Still, you retain enough love to cover
your children with a mother's care

Black woman, my love will cover you,
but I promise to never smother you
Neither will I try to stop your dream,
but I'll make your dream mine too

Black woman, you're a selfless giver
though you have no time to spare
And in those times when others call
on you, your love is always there

Black woman, you continue to trust in
God though the way often gets hard
You will receive your honor here on
earth, but heaven is your just reward

Our Skin Color Goes Deep

"She's high yellow" or "She's pretty for a dark-skinned girl." Or "That brother is so black he looks blue."

Words spoken by us to degrade each other
if our skin color is a certain shade or hue.

We keep ourselves polarized by labeling
some as being too black or not black enough

When will we say enough is enough and stop
binding each other with these colorism cuffs?

The truth is it doesn't matter if you're the deepest
black, damn near white, or anything in between

The world still sees us as people to fear like
Michael Myers in the movie Halloween

Stop bleaching us and teaching us it's
wrong to be too yellow or black

Then start leading us and feeding us
the truth of the matter: it's a fact, that

Before diamonds are transformed by time and
pressure, they begin as a black lump of coal

And the melanin rich yellow and brown skin
we live in is the first cousin to pure gold

Just like diamonds and gold, our value is so
rare that we've been bought, traded, and sold

Our worth has been the single greatest creator
of wealth, despite what we've been told

Because our skin color is just a thin cover that guards the
treasure within our souls, If you dig a lot deeper and go beneath
the surface, you'll discover fine diamonds and pure gold

Mask on, Mask off

The reason I wear a mask over my nose
and mouth is to protect you, not me

It's uncomfortable, it gets in the way and
sometimes is makes it hard to breathe

But if I can't be selfless enough to wear
a mask to protect the one I call my neighbor

Then how I can profess to know Jesus Christ,
the one I call my Lord and Savior

Yet there are so many that profess to know
Jesus and they say it with a smile

But could care less if another soul dies,
cause wearing a mask cramps their style

You can preach all day long about how
you have the blessings of the Lord

But now when you preach Jesus is the way,
I'm looking at you real hard

Because actions speak louder than words
and you have the volume turned on max

You may let Jesus roll off your lips, but your
heart clearly shows your selfish acts

But, the mask of Christianity fits you so
well and you wear it proud and bold

Despite that mask disguising your hateful heart,
your actions reveal an ugly soul

So don't preach to me anymore about how
much you love God and man

Your mask has come down to reveal your
face and it looks a lot like Satan

Mask on, mask off! Whether it's literal or
spiritual, you can take it or leave it

But whether you wear a mask or take it off,
it reveals the truth or conceals it

Faith

God – The First Spoken Word Artist
Songbird
Making Melody in My Heart
No Tears Left for Tomorrow
When My Soul Is Quiet
Transcendent Love
Holy Spirit

God — The First Spoken Word Artist

In the beginning was the Word, and the Word
was with God, and the Word was God.

And then God spoke the words "Let there be..."

His word moved on the face of the deep and darkness
fled, and there in its place stood light instead

One light to illuminate the day, the other to highlight the
night, then God caught a vision and He started to recite

He spat game at the waters until they started to flow, and
He kept right on flowing until dry land started to show

With His own style and rhythm He busted a rhyme
and when God was through He had created time

Then God went freestyle with His lyrics and things
started to get real. He planted the trees of knowledge
and life and formed every beast in the field

He spoke into mankind the breath of life and when
He saw that man was lonely, He gave him a wife

God said I created man to be just like me, so
when His word goes out it won't return empty

So man spoke to the animals and called them by name
and whatever he called them God called them the same

When God was done speaking, He saw that His game was
the truth, then He dropped the mic and said, "That's good!"

Songbird

Sweet little songbird, how beautiful your voice
Your dawn chorus can be heard at the glowing sunrise
All of heaven and earth listen and are entertained
Its beautiful melodies rise far and high into the open air
So expertly crafted and colorful are your notes
Only your profound beauty compares to their splendor
God has touched your voice and given you this gift
What a truly beautiful experience for all that hear it
The Blue Jay, the most handsome of all songbirds, envies you
Like the Cardinal, your range stretches far and wide
The Mockingbird, though it may try cannot mimic your song
The Finch and the Sparrow can only marvel at your sound
Songbird, set your perch high in the tree and sing your song
Sing it from sunrise to dusk; I will never tire of hearing its refrains
Let it wake me in the morning to usher in a brand new day
Let it soothe my mind at night so I may have a peaceful rest
Your song comforts and inspires me to face the challenges ahead
It tells of the glory of God and the awesome power of His might
The wonderful Creator has made you to sing His praise
To cause all those that listen to understand His mind and character
Your jubilant tune recants His mighty
acts displayed through His creation!

Making Melody in My Heart

When the songbird's voice no longer fills
the air because she refuses to sing
And when the clock tower falls silent and
does not chime with its melodious ring

The band just played its last song of the night
and all the music stops
At the early morn when all is calm before
the sun evaporates the dew drops

I speak to myself in psalms and hymns and
meditate on God's Word
Singing those spiritual songs and making
melody in my heart to the Lord

No Tears Left for Tomorrow

It's You, Lord, who hears my cries and
catches all the tears I weep
And Your ointment soothes my swollen eyes
while I'm still asleep

Throughout the night I drown in a
pillow of hopelessness and sorrow
Your Word has promised to replace
my pain with Your joy on tomorrow

Tonight, I count the stars to number
my troubles beneath the darkened skies
But at dawn, the sun rises and evaporates
the dew from my dampened eyes

Before the night gives way to morning,
I will have cried all my tears
In the still of the night, heavenly hosts
arrived and subdued my inner fears

Last night, Your voice comforted me
and allowed my soul to rest in peace
Today, I wake to the voice of the songbird
singing praise that will never cease

Its melody reminds me that because of
You, I awoke with a second chance
To praise You because of who You are
regardless of my circumstance

When My Soul Is Quiet

There's no sound of crickets chirping,
interrupting the silence of the night
And I scan my heart for my favorite melody,
but it appears to have taken flight

No annoying tune is stuck in my head
and even my thoughts refuse to speak
When my footsteps, though crossing
the wooden floor, won't cause it to creak

Even when I summon my poet's voice,
he speaks not even a mumbling word
And though I tune my ear to hear, not even
the whisper of my inner voice is heard

That's when I know I must lift my eyes
to the hills, then turn and seek God's face
For it's only He who can save me from
the silence and carry me to a safe place

Transcendent Love

Our love for you goes beyond the bounds
of the physical human experience
As you shine brightly on us from on high,
we view your star from a distance

Dearly beloved, though you have departed
this life and transitioned into abundant life
Your example of love is incomparable and
exceeded only by the love of Christ

Neither death nor life or anything in
creation can separate us from your love
For your love transcends the limits of the
universe while you sit in heaven above

But your presence is missed daily, and there
are some days that are just too hard
Our peace is knowing your absence from us
is evidence of your presence with God

Your legacy of love will always remain and
continues to inspire us to reach higher
By your love, our lives have been shaped
and shape the lives of all we encounter

Not many days pass that we're not
reminded of things you used to say or do
It's those memories that give us pause
and peace when we think of you

Holy Spirit

You are the third person in the Trinity and
have been here since God said, "Let us..."
Though we readily acknowledge, as we should,
God the Father and the Son, Jesus

We oftentimes forget that You're the
One God sent to this world to keep us
You're there when we can't seem to pray
as we should, and You intercede to God for us

And when we hear the Word but can't
comprehend, You're always there to teach us
It's You who speaks directly with God
when God's Word needs to reach us

When we find ourselves at a loss for
words, it's You who comes to speak for us
And when we pray and miracles are displayed,
it's Your power working within us

When Jesus returns for the believers,
He will know us because You have sealed us
Although we don't always make You feel
welcome, Your presence is ever with us

Holy Spirit, fall afresh and reveal the right that lies within us
It is by Your power we are called to witness
and to do the work God placed in us

Struggle

Pieces of Me
Life's Struggles
The Best Part of Me
I Had a Fight with a Man
2018
Just One Chance
Black Friday
So Much Better

Pieces of Me

I've written poems about sunsets and sunrises. And some have been about the travails of life's painful regrets

I've written poems about wonderful memories from the past and others about memories I would rather forget

I've written my share of poems about love and romance and many have captured the emotions of betrayal and trust

And sometimes, I write poetry about erotica and desire that's meant to tease the mind with sex and lust

Poetry paints a picture to let the heart feel and allow the mind to see. It reveals what is real, not what you would like it to be

All in life is a poem and poetry is about truth. My poetry tells the stories of events and thoughts that make up the pieces of me

Life's Struggles

Sometimes life hits hard, slaps me right in the face
My hands down by my side didn't have time to duck or brace

Feeling dizzy, head spinning, but I can't fall on my face
I'm bruised, dazed, and confused as I try to retrace

The footsteps of my journey that brought me to this time and space
But I got to keep my mind sane as I come face to face

With the struggles of my past still giving me chase
Feet don't fail me now because I'm trying to stay in the race

Head pounding, heart racing, I can hardly keep up the pace
I'm trying to move forward, but I find myself running in place

Would have stopped a long time ago but for God's amazing grace
I can't see myself finishing, but I'm trying to embrace

All the good that God has for me as He tries to replace
Everything I lost due to shame and disgrace

All He wants in return is for me to give Him His rightful place

The Best Part of Me

It's hard moving forward without the one I called my queen
It's even harder looking back at the way things could have been

I had a picture-perfect life with a beautiful wife
And the love of two children to fill up our lives

Blessed with the dream home and money in my pocket
Career on the fast track, taking flight like a rocket

But somehow in the middle of this fairy tale story
We lost track of God and failed to give Him the glory

Now, the world I knew came crashing down at my feet
Never thought in my lifetime I would feel such defeat

The one you love most is the one who causes the worst hurt
I feel like I died inside but don't cover me with dirt

Broken pieces all over the ground leave a trail a mile long
So hard to move forward when the best part of me is gone

I Had a Fight with a Man

Last night, I fought a man, and he fought back with all his might
And we jostled and struggled together for the duration of the night

I resisted him with all I had but couldn't gain the upper hand
I took a step back in awe to wonder, who is this strong man?

I saw the silhouette of his face cast against the filtered moonlight
It was the face of a stranger that I didn't recognize at first sight

We seemed to be about the same size and same height
And I knew our strength was equal, so I settled in for a long fight

He hit so hard and fast, and one blow caught me right in the eye
The pain was so great that I realized, one of us would have to die

We matched each other's skills strike for strike and blow for blow
Neither of us would give any ground but stood toe to toe

He proved to be a worthy opponent and his skills were very elite
But if death is to greet one of us then he and death would meet

We fought so hard and long, I wondered if this would be my end
I tried every kick and punch I knew, but his will would not bend.

And just as my strength had left me, and I thought that I would die
I woke from this nightmare only to realize that other man was I

2018

New Year
New Day
Lord, I'm praying I find my way

Setting goals
Not resolutions
For every problem, I've got solutions

Gonna reap
All I've sown
Claiming this year as my own

There's no mountain
I won't climb
I'll reach the summit in due time

Old burdens
Are cast away
This year I'll see a brighter day

Just One Chance

Just one chance is all I ask and that's not asking a lot
A chance to find my place in this world and give to it all I've got

A chance to be me
A chance to freelance
A chance to do things my own way

A chance to love
A chance for romance
A chance to choose to go or stay

A chance to believe
A chance to forgive
A chance to understand why I pray

A chance to advance
A chance to achieve
A chance for my life to be on display

A chance to live
A chance to die
A chance to grow old and gray

A chance to learn
A chance to dream
A chance to become whom I may

A chance to enhance
A chance to give back
A chance to make someone's day

A chance to fail
A chance to succeed
A chance to start afresh today

A chance to lead
A chance to follow
A chance to grow wiser each day

Instead of giving me a hard way to go, please, just give me a chance

Black Friday

It's beginning to look a lot like Christmas everywhere you go

Christmas bells ringing, carolers singing,
and lovers are kissing under the mistletoe

People searching trying to find that last toy,
panicking because there's none left on the shelf

Mindless bodies just going through the motion,
blindly serving as agents of the jolly old elf

Folks spending money like it grows on trees,
while bank balances are falling like dead leaves

The store manager is smiling as he hears the cash register
cha- chinging and the cashier shouts, "Come again, please!"

Look there's a fight on the big screen TV aisle. Granny
got mad and threw that store attendant a mile

I guess Christmas will be late this year because Santa just
got body slammed. Looks like he'll be laid up for a while!

So Much Better

You will find that life becomes so much better,
when you remain true to your self

Then start living your life to your own truth,
and not to the truth of someone else

Scale your own mountains! It's so much better,
though the air is harder to breathe

But the air you breathe is just that much fresher,
if you're out front taking the lead

Achieve your own goals! It's much more rewarding,
than you just being a dreamer

When you bake your own cake and eat it too,
it tastes just a little more sweeter

That fire inside you, it burns a whole a lot hotter,
when the fire is started by you

And when the fire gets too hot, while everyone faints,
its light leads you through

When Two Become One
"I Do," Again
Can Two Walk Together?
Today, I Saw Love
Thinking of You
Chocolate Valentine
Secrets
The Sugar
The Answer

When Two Become One

When two people in love choose to be one,
A knot is tied that can never be undone.
Two families are united and another formed,
As love creates an eternal bond.

Holy vows are exchanged as all bear witness,
This contract to love that's sealed with a kiss.
The ring is symbolic with its unbroken shape,
Of the continuous love that marriage partakes.

When a man and a woman have chosen to love,
God's blessings rain down from heaven above.
A union is formed that can only compare,
To the union with God, in which they both share.

Two hearts, two minds, two souls entwine,
Dedicated to each other for a lifetime.
United through wedlock with one accord,
Helping each other to grow in the Lord.

The first day of the beginning of a life together,
A life sharing the future for worst or better.
A new life of growing together is born,
When two people in love become one.

"I do," Again

It seems like only yesterday when we first made our holy vows
Time seems to have held its place to preserve the very hour

Although many years have passed, and our youthfulness is gone
The love we share has no less bliss than when it first began

Because His love covered us when the clouds began to form
Our love has passed the test of time and weathered every storm

His strength has lifted us in those times when things went wrong
And through it all, we endured and watched our love grow strong

The Lord has chosen to bless us thrice with fruit of the womb
Which filled our hearts with joy and made our house a home

And in these wonderful years gone by our love has never changed
A marriage as great as the one we have is worth doing again

With God and you as our witnesses, we turn back the hands of time
So that we may pledge our love anew and say our vows a second time

Today, we're still persuaded the vows we made then were true
And to every promise made in our youth the answer is still "I do"

Can Two Walk Together?

How can two walk together for fifty years
unless they first choose to agree?
To show love for each other as much at
seventy as they did at twenty-three

Agree to honor and respect each other
from the first day of marriage until forever
To show each other that the words "I do"
mean that I will for worse or better

Agree to climb life's stairs together, rather
than ride the elevator to the top alone
To hold each other's dreams in the palms
of both hands and claim them as your own

Agree to weather the turbulent storms
whenever those dark clouds arise
To always pray together and ask God
for guidance until the blue skies arrive

Agree to walk together in faith, rather than
walk blindly though having 20/20 sight
To trust that God's grace is enough to
sustain us and not trust in our own might

Agree that the road that's traveled the
least is the one God designed for us
Assured that beyond the bumpy and dusty
road, a street paved with gold awaits us

Agree that when our marriage has turned
50, our love will remain forever young
Though half a century may appear to be
an eternity, our love has just begun

Agree that as we enter our golden days,
our golden years will give us more
More of the same blessings that God
has given to us in the fifty years before

Agree that our journey won't end at fifty
but will last until the last breath we breathe
For our walk is blessed and highly favored
because the two of us chose to agree

Today I Saw Love

As I pulled into the parking lot, my eyes caught
this couple as they left a restaurant

For some unknown reason, I felt compelled to watch
before I left my car to take care of my business

It wasn't because they were fashionably dressed or stood out due
to outward beauty. They were actually dressed pretty shabby

She didn't have a body like an hourglass but had on
shorts that showed the cellulite on her thighs and legs

He wasn't tall with good looks but had thinning
hair with a bald spot in the back and a beer gut

They were devoid of all the superficial
and artificial things we define as beauty

I watched as they held hands as he walked her across the street

And as she stepped off the curb he supported
her arm to make sure she didn't fall or trip

When they got to her car they embraced, and he gave her a
passionate kiss, which they held for about a minute

And at the end of the kiss and before they said their
goodbyes, they looked deep into each other's eyes

I don't recall their lips moving to say any words

She then rubbed his back and he grabbed her ass;
they said good-bye, got into their cars, and departed

Love has nothing to do with how beautiful you look. It's how beautiful you make each other feel about yourselves

That's what makes love such a wonderful thing

Thinking of You

Countless times I think of you in the passing of a day
My heart fills with joy as thoughts of you are ushered my way

Refreshing thoughts, warm and pure, kindling my love for you anew
Precious thoughts remind me each
day of how much I really miss you

Neither distance nor time can separate the love we share
So long as thoughts of you, my darling, always linger in the air

Nothing can interfere with the perfect love that abides
As long as God's divine hand directs, leads, and guides

A phone call or letter is a substitute, but nothing can ever replace
The sweetness of your loving kiss and warmness of your embrace

The time grows closer as one day ends and a brand new one starts
Soon we'll be together forever, never again to depart

Until that day is here at last, these thoughts I'll hold so true
Remember in those times that you
feel alone, I'm always thinking of you

Chocolate Valentine

Chocolate, how much do I crave your taste?
You excite my heart and cause it to race
Yet, still so soothing, like a warm embrace
Indulgence in you puts a smile on my face

Chocolate lips dipped in Hershey kisses
Those alluring eyes expose my weakness
My mind is consumed by your sweetness
My heart stolen, you leave me breathless

I extend my hand to touch your skin
Dark, rich chocolate, smooth as satin
More pleasant than I could ever imagine
Flows through my fingers like a fountain

Many assorted candies, but it's you I favor
My mouth waters for your distinct flavor
The taste of your love, I relish and savor
My desire for you will never waiver

Dipped in chocolate down to your feet
Frosted and swirled a delicious treat
The quality of your taste, oh, so sweet
A simple pleasure that I must repeat

Secrets

Each day I write your secrets on my heart
Secrets you've only shared with me
I'll keep them locked away safely
These secrets you've shared I'll never tell.

Only you have the matching key
That reveals the treasure, which lies within
No one else can view its wealth
Hidden in my heart I'll guard them well.

New nuggets that you reveal each day
I'll protect them like a chest of gold
Never to be revealed to any soul
Every intruder I will repel.

So many secrets we've exchanged
That overflow their walls and fall to the floor
No stranger can force me to give up this treasure
No matter how hard he compels.

Tell me your heart and I'll share mine
I'll keep its secrets until time is no more
Your secrets have become mine
These secrets you've shared I'll never tell.

The Sugar

Your dark skin is so sweet to my taste, just
like chocolate cake fresh from the baker
You got my chest pounding and heartbeat
racing; I'm gonna need to get a pacemaker

Your sexy chocolate leaves me breathless
as I whisper sweet nothings in your ear
But I don't want any artificial sweetener,
only unadulterated sugar served here

You're my drug dealer, and I'm your
addict, the sole source of my affliction
And your sweetness is both the cause
and the cure, for my comatose condition

Got your arms locked around my neck
so tight, acting like you been missing me
Your doughnut glazed lips are glued to
mine; I'm loving the way you're kissing me

My weakness is in my addiction to you,
and I need you to be my candy pusher
You're toxic, so I can't keep feasting on you,
cause you gonna give me "The Sugar"!

The Answer

Has the season for love passed me by or
should I repent and give love another try?
Will I hold my position of resist and deflect
or when love calls my name will I reply?

Will I give love a second chance or should
I build a great wall of resistance?
Can I feel the power of love again or will I
only view it in others from a distance?

Should my arms only hold on to emptiness
or will I find someone special to embrace?
Will honey be the only sweetness my lips will
taste or will honeydew lips take its place?

Will I ever find the kind of love, which
touches that place deep in my soul?
Or will I continue to find 24-carat nuggets,
only to discover in the end its fool's gold?

Will I find that special someone to show
love through my time, words, and deeds?
Or will past disappointments keep me
from the one who answers all my needs?

I found the answer to all these questions
when I met you, the woman of my dreams
Now my faith in love has been restored,
for in you, I found hope again it seems

You are the answer to the loneliness that
held my heart captive for far too long
You opened the door and freed my heart
to passion I thought was long gone

You are the answer to the bitter taste
a hurtful relationship leaves behind
And your presence replaced my bitterness
with sweetness over the course of time

You are the answer to help heal the scars
that keep me from the best version of me
For you looked past my flaws and saw
in me, the person you knew I could be

Through you, I learned how to love again,
and these arms are empty no more
And when we make love, my soul remembers,
just how good love was before

My heart is grateful you made me feel
whole again, and it's reflected in all I do
And for every question presented to me,
I found the answer, when I found you.

Family

Family Reunion
A Poem Just for You (Monica Copprue)
You Taught Me to Be a Dad
My Little Princess
Your Mother and I
Mother Dear (Madea)
"My Daddy"
Thank You, Brother

Family Reunion

It's time again to head down south to the Williams' family reunion
To a familiar place from yesterday, filled with so much laughter and fun
Where the fields are wide and spacious, with plenty of room to run

Reflecting on a time that's passed, where you could live the simple life
A time that was pure and innocent, absent from struggle and strife
Where the pine trees grow tall and straight and stretch toward the sky

We will come together on Clara Williams Road
at the little house that sits on a hill
To sit on the porch, wiping sweat from our brows,
on a summer night so hot and still
Listening for the sound of the night owl,
the Bob White and the whippoorwill

Overeating until our stomachs are full from
the buffet of Madea's delicious food
While we reminisce about the good old days—
both the bad and the good
Laughing about a whooping we got from
Dad just for forgetting to cut firewood

Family customs and traditions are being
repeated and passed down to the grands
And Daddy always reminds us we need to
give honor to God with praying hands
The memories will fade as time has passed,
but our family's love it still stands

A Poem Just for You (Monica Copprue)

Many heart-warming thoughts dance rapidly through my mind, as I think of a poem about you

Only once we've met; yet, I'm so utterly impressed until depicting you in poetry was very easy to do

Now, I know first impressions are often deceiving, but this image of you, I believe to be true

Interesting, intriguing, and attractive to say the least, traits that are only the beginning when it comes to you

Charming, loving, tender, and true. Kind, considerate, and sweet, just to name a few

A virtuous woman whose price is far above rubies, diamonds, pearls, and precious metals too

Chaste and pure, a woman who truly loves the Lord, given to holiness, willing to go all the way through

Open-minded and flexible, adaptative to change. Confident of your abilities, not afraid of things that are new

Personable, perceptive, sensitive to others' needs. Always knowing just the right thing to say and do

Probably now, as you've read carefully through, you've consented that all of the above is both accurate and true

Rarely is it that a guy meets a woman like you, who is beautiful on the outside and inside too

Usually, her inward conceitedness contrasts her outward beauty, but I don't detect that at all from you

Each word I've used is not vanity I'm sure, but an accurate portrait of Monica Copprue

You Taught Me to Be a Dad

Son, on the day you were born, life as a father began for me.
It was then that we set out on a journey that will last forever.

From the first day we met, I wanted you to be a better version
of me. But I realized the best version of you is so much better.

And how could I teach you to become a man while learning to be
one myself? So we would learn the lessons of life together.

We have traveled some roads that are not easy to travel, but instead
of following the trends, son, we became the trendsetters.

I taught you all I knew about the many nuances of life. While
seeing life through the innocence of a little boy's eyes.

I taught you to be honest and a man of your word. That when
you find yourself in a tough spot, the truth is greater than lies.

I taught you about character and having the courage to do
the right thing, even though no one else is around to see it.

I taught you to be your own man, to follow your own path and
dreams, to choose who you want to become in life, then be it.

I taught you that no one should know you better than you
do, to always be true to others, but first, be true to yourself.

I taught you that to be great, you must find your greatness from
within. To never allow your worth to be defined by someone else.

How quickly time has passed as I watched you transform from
a boy into a man. I'm so proud, I can hardly contain myself.

Where did that little boy go who needed me to hold his hand and encourage him he could do things by himself?

As I look in life's mirror and see the reflection of a father and son, I'm proud of the men I see, and it makes my heart glad.

After all this time, I thought it was I who was teaching you to become a man, but it was you who taught me to become a dad.

My Little Princess

As I hold on to your arm, readying myself
to walk you down the aisle
I see a beautiful young woman wrapped
in white linen displaying a radiant smile

But while standing here, I remember your
birthday and the first breaths you drew in
And that first time I held you in my arms,
you were wrapped in only a blanket then

I thought about the little girl I entertained
with the hand puppet show at night
The one I gave piggyback rides to before
we prayed, and I tucked you in tight

The little girl I gave horseback rides,
the one I read fairy tales to
That little girl who believed
there was nothing her daddy couldn't do

I watched you grow into my little princess,
a young lady with a purpose-driven life
A life of singing, dancing, and living,
but most of all, a life in Christ

I remember the night I presented you
to the world at the annual debutante ball
The many traits they sought in a belle,
my daughter, you possess them all

When you left for college to pursue your
dreams, I let you go but held on softly
I knew you could do this on your own and
become the woman you were to be

And I knew the first time I saw you with
him, it was only a matter of time
Though I find it hard to give you away,
I know the two of you will be just fine

I know at the altar I must let you go, but
a place in my heart will always be yours
And I was the first to capture your heart,
since the day you were born

Today, I'm presenting a queen to him
to become his beloved wife
But in my heart, you will always be,
my little girl, my little princess for life

Your Mother and I

It's your mother and I who through conscious
love brought you into this world
And through that love, we were blessed
by God with the gift of a beautiful baby girl

Your mother and I have watched our gift
grow and bless all that cross your path
You reward the lives of all you encounter,
with your ability to love, live, and laugh

Today, your mother and I are voicing our
blessing on this union, not giving you away
We're re-gifting you, to gain a son, so
that you may bless him in the same way

It's your mother and I who are so
overjoyed our joy is impossible to hide
And on your wedding day, we present you
to him, as his beautiful blushing bride

We pray this new union prospers and
is blessed by God as time goes by
By God's gift to us, his life is blessed, but
the most blessed of all, is your mother and I

Mother Dear (Madea)

Madea you left me too soon,
but your legacy is mine to keep
Although the depth of it is hard to follow,
and its slope is very steep

As your son, I'll cherish the memories
of your many selfless deeds
Madea, you never failed
to meet your family's daily needs

You were a selfless giver who always
sought to meet the needs of others
And to many youths in our community,
you were often a second mother

You spoke for me before I had the confidence
to speak up for myself
Your soft-spoken voice encouraged me
when there was no one else

And when I made poor choices or
didn't do what you told me to do
No switch could inflict the pain I felt
when I knew I had disappointed you

You had a way of showing your love
that made me ashamed of my actions
It caused me to change my behavior
in a way that was to your satisfaction

And just as it did before you went
home to be in the arms of the Lord
My heart still seeks to find comfort,
from your timely and seasoned words

My mind still talks to you,
to hear your wisdom and unbiased advice
When I was right you stood by me,
if I was wrong then you would chastise

Even now, the cloudy days still come
when I need your wisdom as a guide
Your words remind me that the glow
in the cloud is the sun shining behind

Madea, the faith you showed me
before you went home to rest
Gave me the example that I will follow
when my faith faces its own test

I know that your home is in heaven now and
you're finally at peace
My peace is in knowing your burden
is over and your soul is now at ease

Madea, you didn't seek fortune or
fame but was rich in faith and love
Your spirit lives on in those you left
and your treasure is in heaven above

"My Daddy"

I watched you as you tuned in to Walter Cronkite
and the 6 p.m. news every day
And the Bible, the South Alabamian,
and Mobile Press were never that far away

Your hunger and thirst for knowledge
is a gift you passed down to me
I'm glad I inherited the best part of you;
it's a treasure I'll always keep

With your broad shoulders, you laid a solid
foundation on which I could build my life
If not for those shoulders for me to stand
on I couldn't have set my goals so high

Had you not taught me the value of hard
work, I would be hungry many a day
And without those valuable life lessons,
I wouldn't be the man I am today

In spite of the prejudices you were
subjected to, you chose not to be bitter
You selflessly endured the hardness of
this life, so that my life would be better

You gave up all to protect your family
and were willing to pay the ultimate price
Only when I became older and wiser
did I realize your great sacrifice

Your mind was as strong as a steel trap,
and you had the courage of a lion
Your will to help others was sturdy as
a rock with the consistency of pure iron

You loved this land between Slaughter
Bend and Gopher Hill more than wealth
The love you had for this community
remained, even as you lost your health

Your legacy won't be soon forgotten,
just because you're no longer here
You're a mason, preacher, community
organizer, and civil rights pioneer

We will miss your many lessons
on all things pertaining to history
But what we will miss most of all,
we will miss you, "My Daddy"

Thank You, Brother

I was young, but I remember the visit to our house by the FBI
And I'll never forget the black and white photo of you with a black eye
Thank you, brother, for your bravery that day

You had the courage to stand when
lesser men would have taken flight
While others fell before the terror of racists,
you stood for what was right
Because of the sacrifices you made, I am free today

You are what heroes are made of,
the stuff you can't buy, steal, or teach
Your valor is just too far beyond us mere mortals' reach
Thank you, brother, for being my hero that day

You were the foot soldier on the frontline
that set the course for me to follow
You fought for freedom then so that I could walk in it tomorrow
Thank you, brother! I owe you a debt I could never repay

Thank you always, Clyde!

Relationship

Naked
First Impressions
Material Stuff
What's on Your Mind?
Beautiful, Bold, and Confident
Someone Like You
A Smile as Lovely as a Poem

Naked

When I am comfortable standing before you
with all my imperfections disrobed
When I am safe lying next to you
with all my insecurities exposed

When I am confident the secrets
I shared with you will never be told
When I am convinced your love for me
will grow stronger and never old

When I am persuaded you won't laugh
when I reveal my dreams to you
When I am sure you won't exploit my
weaknesses, though it's very easy to do

When I am assured if I put away my mask
and allow you to see my tears
When I am certain I can reveal the truth
about my most crippling fears

Then I will be positive we have the kind
of trust derived from the naked truth
And will achieve the intimacy we both
desire and the passion it unlooses

First Impressions

We've met only once, but you put your stamp on my mind
Though my head always knows the truth, my heart is legally blind

The mental image I formed of you, is it true or what I want it to be?
Will I trust what my heart feels or will I trust what my eyes see?

My heart sees the best in you cause I'm all caught up in how I feel
But feelings are like a mirage in the desert; they aren't always real

Do I turn a blind eye to the truth that your actions clearly show?
Or do I believe the lie my heart tells me
because I just don't want to know

Is it live or is it memorex? Should I
press pause or should I press play?
This sounds like a song I've played before,
but will I let my heart rule the day?

At first sight, you always seem to be
the one, my one and only ride or die
But just when I think you are the truth, you turn out to be that lie

Appearances are deceitful and often dress up in a disguise
Just when I thought I had you figured out, guess what? Surprise!

Material Stuff

I own a Rolex, but if I didn't, would you still give me the time of day?
Or would you be dismissive and send me on my merry way?

I drive a Mercedes, but if I didn't, would you ride with me still?
Or leave me in the middle of the road like fresh road kill?

If you didn't know I've lived in mansions or visited Paris in spring
Would I still be the one you want to make your main thing?

If I give you all I have, but I may not be rich enough
Would I still be your man or are you hung up on material stuff?

What's On Your Mind?

If you ain't feeling me right now then
stop tripping and be real with me
Don't leave me wondering how you
feel if you don't wanna deal with me

Don't cause me to be a psychic and have to read your mind
That's a setup for failure, and I'm gonna fail you every time

Please tell me everything you need, and I'll give you what you want
You know I aim to please you, so let me know when I don't

I promise to keep it real while your so-called friends are fronting on you
I'm staying steady as steel, so I ain't stunting on you

Beautiful, Bold, and Confident

She enters the room and silence falls as the men all pause in dismay
Awed by the confidence in her walk and the way her hips gently sway

All eyes in the room follow her as she so elegantly finds her way
As the scent from her Dolce and Gabbana fragrance leads the way

Her smile, it's so radiant you can see it from a great distance away
It shines so brightly it makes the darkest night appear as noonday

Her personality is so vivid it paints with colors bold and gay
And her style, it's so colorful it makes other women fade to gray

Her inner confidence speaks boldly as men ponder her name and say
She's beautiful, bold, and confident, and I hope she comes my way

Someone Like You

Someone like you whose skin is as soft as newly spun
silk and as refreshing as the rain from an April shower

Someone like you whose perfume bombards the air
with the pleasant aroma of freshly cut flowers

Someone like you whose embrace is as warm as summer
and whose kiss is moist as the early morning dew

Someone like you whose loyalty warrants the love of
that special someone who proves they are worthy of you

Someone like you whose style captures the imagination,
while dressed in red-bottomed pumps and pink pearls

Someone like you who is the object of men's affection
and the muse of your sisters and all the other girls

Someone like you whose love is so passionate and fierce
as that of a mother bear protecting her young cub

Someone like you who has smiled through your tears and
remained strong when lesser souls would have succumbed

Someone like you who has conquered your fears,
while still standing strong for the ones you cover

Someone like you whose spirit remains as sweet as
honey, despite the bitterness that this life has to offer

Someone like you whose heart is as pure as 24-carat
gold and has the innocence of the first winter snowfall

Someone like you whose faith is always so sure because
your trust lies in the only one who controls it all

If my heart could find the one love that will always
be true, then I will find it with someone like you!

A Smile as Lovely as a Poem

It's not the sexiness in your walk or the curve of your hips that excite me but the pleased expression of your infinite smile.

Just like a poem, your smile is my lyrical muse and the words flow so easily to the tempo of its rhythm and style.

Poetry is your smile and your smile is poetic and when beheld in life's perfect mirror, it reflects your inner thoughts.

I feel the mood of your smile as you tell me your dreams and listening to the cadence of your voice arouses my wants.

The perfect shape of your smile causes the corner of your lips to curl up, and your eyes, they narrow and squint.

The quality of its beauty holds the characteristics of poetry and is crafted with a measure of purpose and intent.

Your infectious smile is sculpted from pure ivory and cast against a soft background of an ebony hue.

It's accented by the fragrance of Coco Mademoiselle perfume and is as refreshing as the morning dew.

A picturesque smile framed by soft, flowing hair and like a ballad, it follows the sound of a comforting beat.

It's a fond recitation stored in the depths of my memory and like a sweetly phrased sonnet it's worthy to repeat.

Humor

The Funk Is Real
Boy Bye! (Sean Spicer)
A Glass of Wine/a Shot/a Keg of Beer
People Watching

The Funk Is Real

Music bumping that uptown funk appeal,
heads bobbing, and it's bout to get real
So release your mind and let the funk move ya.
Get ready for the great funk reveal

Funk so bold it's bout to take over; you
can take my mind but don't touch my soul
Lights strobing as I step to the dance floor;
I can't turn back bout to lose control

I'm lifted so high and I can't come down;
gonna leave all my troubles behind
My mind's gone from sipping on the juice
from this funk encounter of the third kind

Body pulsating like I done lost my mind;
I can't hide cause the funk is everywhere
It's so strong until I can't stay sober.
I can smell the stench of the funk in the air

Bout to take this trip to the end of the rainbow,
tryna find my funkadelic treasure
Catching a ride on the rhythm of the bass line.
Destination, funkadelic pleasure!

I can hear it coming, so wait for it,
hear the sound of the lead guitar solo riff
Body swaying, my mind playing games with it;
I feel my soul as it starts to drift

Move your body babe, but hold on to your mini;
let the music take us to funky town
I see you feeling the beat and rocking to boogie,
so go on girl let your hair down

Go ahead and let the funk tease your mind.
I promise you won't regret it
Come aboard and enjoy this funkadelic experience;
you won't soon forget it

Boy Bye! (Sean Spicer)

Goodbye Sean Spicer, you know it was only a matter of time
Before your puppet master, Trump, would fire your lying behind

Tell me! How was it to be the mouthpiece of a crazy man?
I'm sure there were days when you wished
you could trade places with KellyAnne

Thank you for a job well done as the communications misdirector
But your official title should have been,
the "Alternative Facts" corrector

It's too bad! You had just mastered the art of the "Shuck and Jive"
Man! We gonna miss your character on Saturday Night Live

So go ahead, Mr. Spicer; take your bow then exit stage right
Thanks to your loyalty to the "Orange One," your career just took a hike

Boy Bye! You can't even go back home
to your friends in the Republican Party!
Maybe you can apply on SNL and
play the role of Melissa McCarthy

A Glass of Wine/a Shot/a Keg of Beer

I'm out for a night on the town in a foreign
land waiting for a cab at the taxi stand
I'm headed on a mission to quench my thirst,
but I'm trying to get my bearings first
If in Italy out on the Etruscan trail, then
a glass of Chianti wine is what sets my sail
If it's Germany, I'm off to the Hofbrauhaus pub,
where a keg of beer is what I love
If I find myself on a Russian plot, then a shot of vodka hits the spot

People Watching

Watching people, and them watching me
Wondering who might they be
And sometimes it's quite a sight to see

I'm wondering, how was your day?
Did it go your way?
Or did something cause it all to go astray?

People just minding their own affairs
Some have long faces with blank stares
She's wearing clothes catching all the glares

Some are just starting their work day
Others off work and are headed to play
Still others are just trying to find their way

There are many who seem in a hurry
Some don't seem to have a single worry
There are a few filled with anger and fury

Occasionally a parent becomes undone
Cause their children are always on the run
People watching is so much fun

www.ingramcontent.com/pod-product-compliance
Lightning Source LLC
LaVergne TN
LVHW051510070426
835507LV00022B/3024